HUMVEES

by Janet Piehl

Lerner Publications Company • Minneapolis

For the Kowalski brothers

Special thanks to Rick Lammers of Bergstrom Hummer in Madison, Wisconsin

Humvee is a registered trademark of AM General LLC. HUMMER is a registered trademark of General Motors Corporation.

Text copyright © 2006 by Janet Piehl

Lerner Publications Company
A division of Lerner Publishing Group
241 First Avenue North
Minneapolis, MN 55401 U.S.A.

Website address: www.lernerbooks.com

Library of Congress Cataloging-in-Publication Data

Piehl, Janet.
        Humvees / by Janet Piehl.
            p.   cm. – (Pull ahead books)
        Includes index.
        ISBN-13: 978-0-8225-2668-1 (lib. bdg. : alk. paper)
        ISBN-10: 0-8225-2668-9 (lib. bdg. : alk. paper)
        1. Hummer truck. 2. United States—Armed Forces—
    Transportation—History—20th century. I. Title. II. Series.
    UG618.P54 2006
    623.7'4722—dc22   2005004344

Manufactured in the United States of America
1 2 3 4 5 6 – JR – 11 10 09 08 07 06

A Humvee can climb a mountain.

It can cross a desert.

It can swim a river.

Humvees are big and strong. These trucks go all over the world. They go wherever the U.S. **military** goes.

The U.S. military uses Humvees to help protect our country.

The truck's full name is High-Mobility Multipurpose Wheeled Vehicle. But soldiers call the truck "Humvee" for short.

What makes this truck so tough?

It has a big **frame**. The whole truck is
built around the frame.

The frame is wide. The tires are set far apart. This makes the truck hard to flip over.

The frame is high off the ground. High frames help Humvees drive over rocks and rough land.

A Humvee's big tires help it drive over rough land too. The tires have special bumps in them called **tread**. Tread keeps the tires from slipping.

Rumble! Rumble! A Humvee has a big **engine**. The engine makes the truck powerful.

The truck has a strong body. This truck has a covering called **armor**. The armor helps stop bullets.

The doors and roofs come off most Humvees. A **roll bar** on top helps to keep soldiers safe if the truck flips over.

How do soldiers use Humvees?

The trucks haul weapons and
equipment for soldiers.

They carry soldiers from place to place.

They are used for fighting. This truck is carrying a **missile** that can shoot at tanks.

This truck is carrying a smaller gun.

Humvees can be **ambulances**. They carry hurt soldiers to hospitals.

The trucks can go almost anywhere.
They can drive through water and
thick mud.

Sometimes soldiers need Humvees in places they cannot drive to. So they have helicopters bring in the trucks.

Helicopters can carry Humvees from place to place. They safely bring the trucks to the ground.

Then the trucks roll over rough roads
and rocks to do their job.

Humvees help keep the United States safe.

Facts about Humvees

■ The U.S. Army has been using Humvees since 1985.

■ Some people drive trucks that look like Humvees but are not army trucks. They are called Hummers. Have you seen one on the street?

■ Humvees are made of steel and aluminum. They are held together by 2,800 pieces called rivets.

■ These big trucks are 7 feet wide, 15 feet long, and up to 6 feet high. They weigh about 5,200 pounds. That's wider, taller, and almost twice as heavy as a normal car.

■ Can you swim as well as a Humvee? The trucks can safely drive through 2.5 feet of water. Special Humvees can drive through 5 feet of water.

Parts of a Humvee

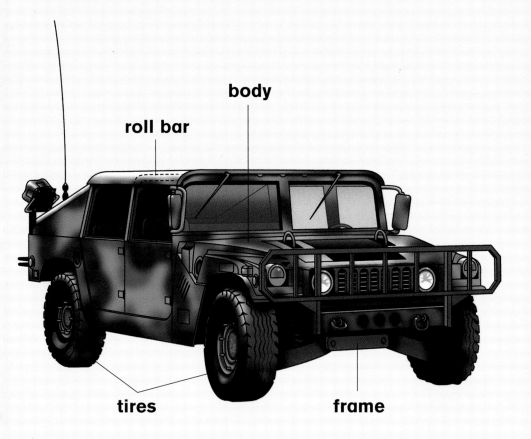

roll bar

body

tires

frame

Glossary

ambulances: cars or trucks that carry hurt people to hospitals. Humvees can be ambulances.

armor: a strong layer that covers the main part of a Humvee. Armor helps stop bullets.

engine: the part that powers a truck

frame: the metal part that the truck's tires and body are placed on

military: a group of men and women who work to protect the United States

missile: a weapon that shoots at far-off objects

roll bar: a metal bar on top of a Humvee. It keeps riders safe if the truck rolls over.

tread: bumps and grooves on a tire

Index

About the Author

Janet Piehl lives in Madison, Wisconsin. To learn about Humvees, she test-drove one of the big trucks. It was very exciting, but she has no plans to buy one—she'd rather ride her bike. She has also written *Formula One Race Cars* and *Chattering Chipmunks*.

Photo Acknowledgments

The photographs in this book appear courtesy of: © AM General, LLC, front cover, pp. 3, 16; © Jim Hollander/Pool/ZUMA Press, p. 4; Horace Murray, U.S. Army, p. 5; Elizabeth Erste, U.S. Department of Defense, p. 6; © Reuters/CORBIS, p. 7; U.S. Marine Corps, pp. 8, 12, 13, 24, 26; U.S. Army, pp. 9, 15, 17, 18, 19, 23, 27; © Stan Honda/AFP/Getty Images, p. 10; April Johnson, U.S. Army, pp. 11, 31; © Matthew Cavanaugh/Getty Images, p. 14; © William Armstrong/U.S. Army/Getty Images, p. 20; William Armstrong/ U.S. Army, p. 21; © AP/Wide World Photos, p. 22. Illustration on p. 29 by Laura Westlund, © Lerner Publishing Group.